Test Pattern

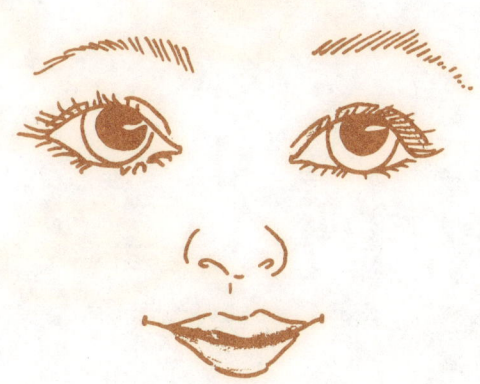

Plate 1

HISTORICAL NOTES & DIRECTIONS

Cloth dolls have been the preferred companions of childhood since the invention of fabric. Today, cloth doll making and collecting is enjoying a resurgence of interest, appealing to "children of all ages." The availability and reasonable cost of the medium, the immensely satisfying results that can be obtained by doll makers of every degree of expertise, and the durability and tactile pleasure derived from the finished product, all combine to maintain its popularity. While it may be impractical for the beginning doll maker to create dolls in other mediums because of the tools, materials, and specialized skills involved, cloth dolls remain well within the range of average abilities and pocketbooks.

The possibilities of fabric must have been instantly apparent to the early doll maker. Textiles are soft and lifelike when compared to bisque, wood and other mediums. One of the earliest examples of fabric dolls was found in the tomb of a little girl of the fourth century. A single blue bead earring that remains on the head, and the large stitches that form the crudely modeled cloth body are silent testimony to the young doll maker of yesterday.

Although cloth dolls have not survived the ravages of time as well as their sturdier counterparts, enough exist to attest to their uninterrupted representation. No period has been entirely without them, and the 19th and 20th centuries provide literally thousands of examples.

For many people the most difficult part of cloth doll making is the design and placement of the facial features. While some dolls are traditionally faceless, such as those made by a few religious groups, or the tiny rolled cloth dolls, most people prefer features to blankness. Doll makers of the past have used various techniques, from delicately oil-painted faces to simple inked-on features, and embroidery and needle-molding methods. Three dimensional effects were often produced by strategically placed objects of assorted sizes and materials beneath the fabric of the face. Pieces of wood shaped "noses" and beans or grains of rice frequently gave form to the "eyes." The edible nature of the latter choices were very attractive to vermin and cloth dolls found with the eye area eaten away were probably made in this manner, and fell victim to some hungry predator.

When an early cloth doll's face became dirty or worn, a new cloth face was often stitched over the old one, and collectors are delighted to find examples of such early "face-lifting." Sometimes the process was repeated several times over the years, and the various layers of faces reflect the changing attitudes of the owners.

Commercially made cloth dolls were available with alternate faces that could be sewn over a worn doll, or simply replaced by preference. These faces slept, cried, smiled and changed moods at the discretion of the owner. Children of other countries and hues could be portrayed in the same manner, with the face changed as easily as the clothing. Cloth doll patterns with alternative faces appeared during the 1880s. The December 1886 issue of *The Delineator* informed the reader that "For small people there are dolls of...muslin, warranted to bear with equanimity the treatment of the exacting little mother." Patterns for the dolls came in seven sizes, for dolls from 12 to 24 inches (30.5 to 61cm) tall, and included three faces. The doll maker was instructed to "use the smallest face for the smallest dolls, the largest faces for the largest dolls and the medium face for the between dolls." The face was to be painted in watercolors, and a "brown false front-piece that was quite curly was sewed on for her hair." In December of 1917 *The Woman's Home Companion* showed an illustration of "a rag doll with a childlike and transferable face...Cut in one size only, eighteen inches high. The face is transferred to the doll with a hot iron." According to the text the doll could be "handled and mishandled at will, for there is nothing destructible about a good old-fashioned rag doll."

Modern doll makers have access to literally thousands of cloth doll books and patterns, but the most difficult part of the process for many people remains the face. A pleasing face can make a simple doll special and a beautifully constructed and sewn doll can be ruined by a poor execution of the features.

This book contains face designs based on some of the most popular types of cloth dolls created in the past and the present. Numerous sizes, expressions and ages are included, as well as instructions for their placement on the head, based on studies of the human figure.

The faces have been printed in brown ink. This unique presentation allows them to be used as is, or elaborated with one or more finishing techniques. Such techniques include oils, pastels, acrylic paints, powdered cosmetics, embroidery, needle-sculpting and base form shaping. The doll maker may add only lip, eye and cheek color to the printed face.

Painting or embroidery techniques are very successful. Remember to use soft delicate

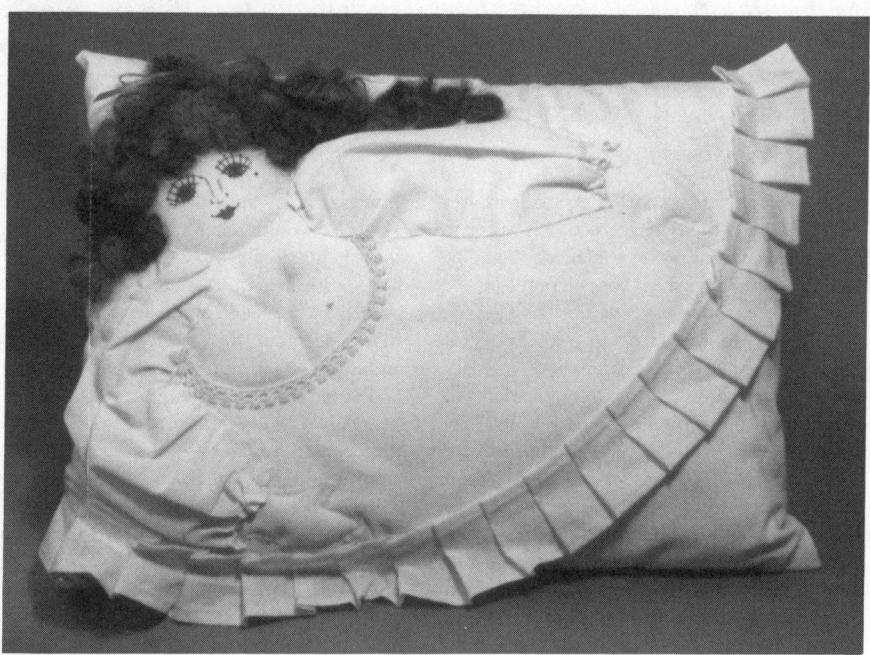

Pillow executed by Rosemary Reus.

Cloth doll pattern and clothing from The Wish Booklets, *designed by Susan Sirkis. Executed by Shawn Rysavy with alternate transfer face.*

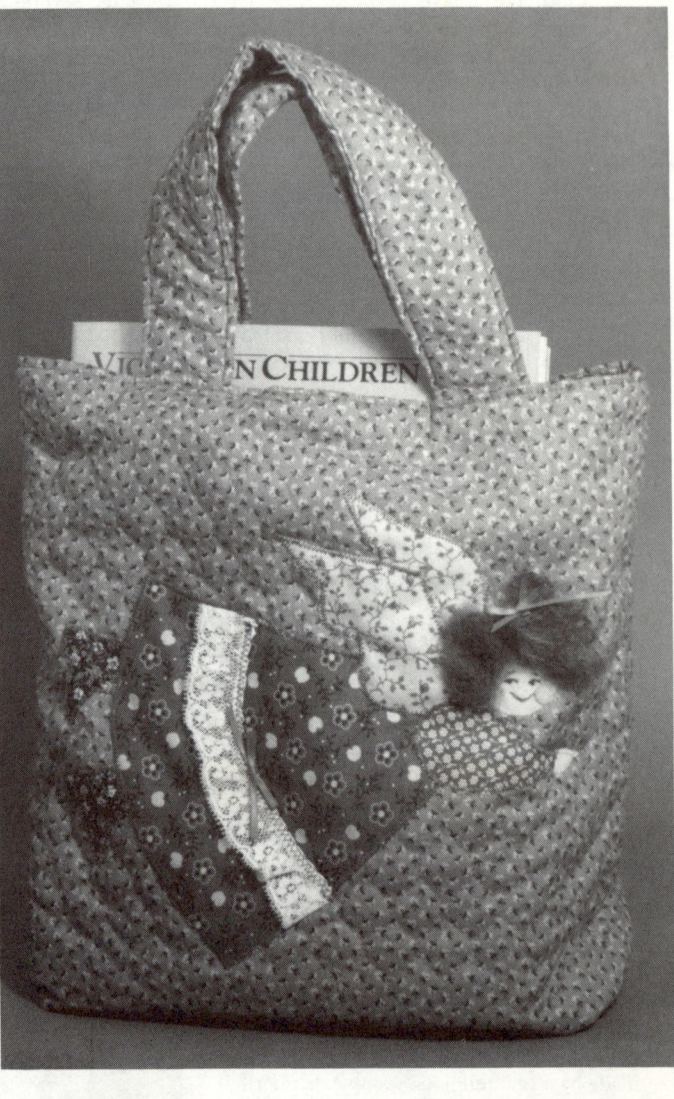

Calico bag with angel design, executed by Rosemary Reus.

hues; a good rule is to use one shade lighter than you think will be correct. It is easier to add color than to remove it. Black should be avoided entirely except for the pupils of the eyes; it is a color that does not truly appear elsewhere on the face, with the possible exception of eyebrows, and tends to make faces (even human ones) look older and coarser. Dark browns are better. Eye and cheek colors should be suitable for the subject, i.e., soft colors and pale rosy tints for babies, and progressively darker, more vivid colors, as the age of the doll indicates. Pastels and powdered cosmetics can be applied with soft brushes, cotton swabs or toothpicks with a wisp of cotton wound around the end, depending on the size of the doll. After application excess color can be brushed away. Remember to gently blush the chin, forehead, earlobes and hairline, as well as the cheeks. You may also add color to the fingertips, elbows, knees, buttocks or any other place where it would occur naturally. When the color is placed as you wish it to be, it can be fixed with a mist of clear plastic spray or unscented non-aersol hair spray. This type of color adds life and character immediately, and is used in combination with embroidery and other finishing techniques.

When using embroidery methods remember to separate the strands of floss according to the size of the doll. Large dolls usually take three strands, small dolls only one. Fine silk thread is excellent for tiny doll faces. When embroidering faces always bury the thread in the stuffing between features so that you will not have a dark line showing beneath the fabric of the "skin" leading from one part of the face to another. If the face is embroidered on a hoop, prior to placing on the doll, each section should be embroidered and the thread secured behind each feature. Knots often show and an alternative is the use of a tiny dot of white milliners glue to secure the end of the thread to the back of the fabric, under the embroidered section. Use the smallest possible amount and let the glue dry completely before removing the face from the hoop.

Combinations of embroidery and painting techniques create wonderful dolls, and both processes may be done on a hoop. Paint all areas desired first. Thinned acrylic watercolors are permanent and pretty. Practice on the fabric you plan to use first, to see what the liquid ratio should be; some fabrics are more absorbent than others. Let paints dry thoroughly before doing needlework. Oil pastels can also be done with the face on a hoop, however they will come off on embroidery thread if care is not taken.

Continued after pattern section.

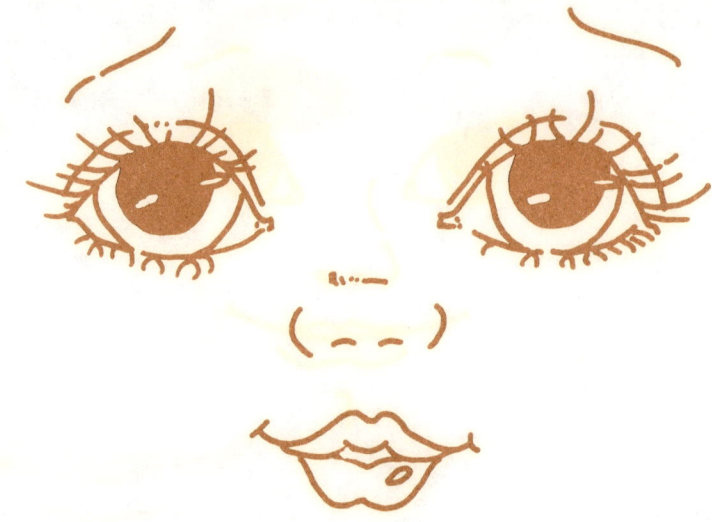

Test Pattern

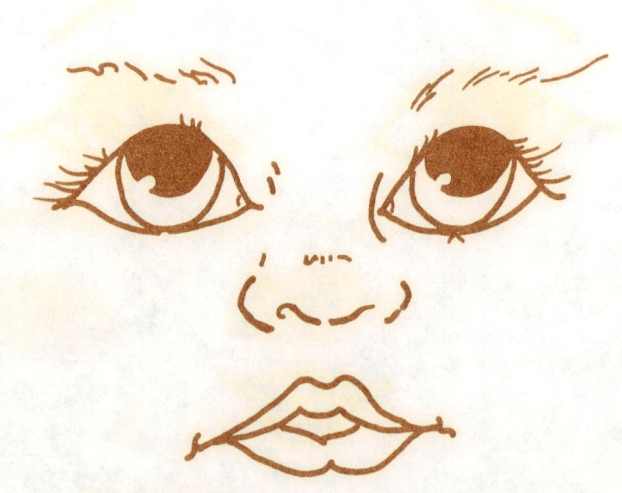

Plate 2

Test Pattern

Plate 3

Plate 4

Test Pattern

Test Pattern

Plate 5

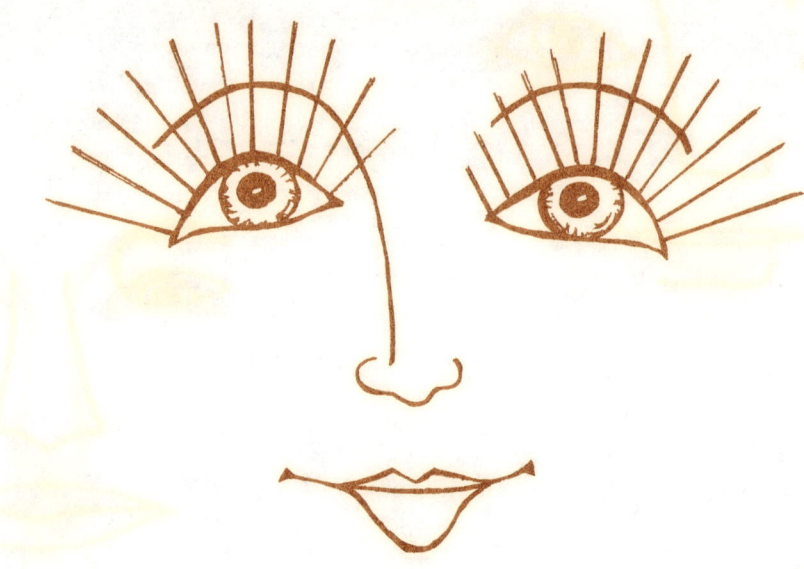

Test Pattern

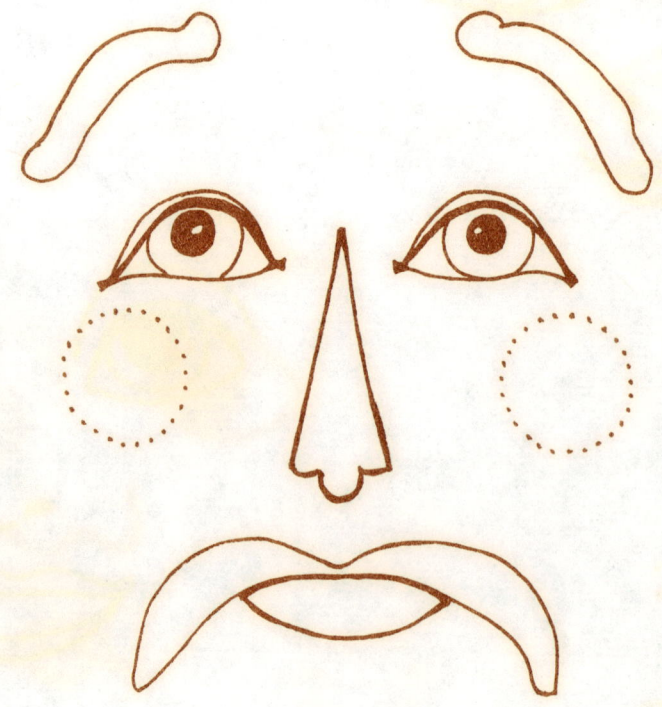

Plate 6

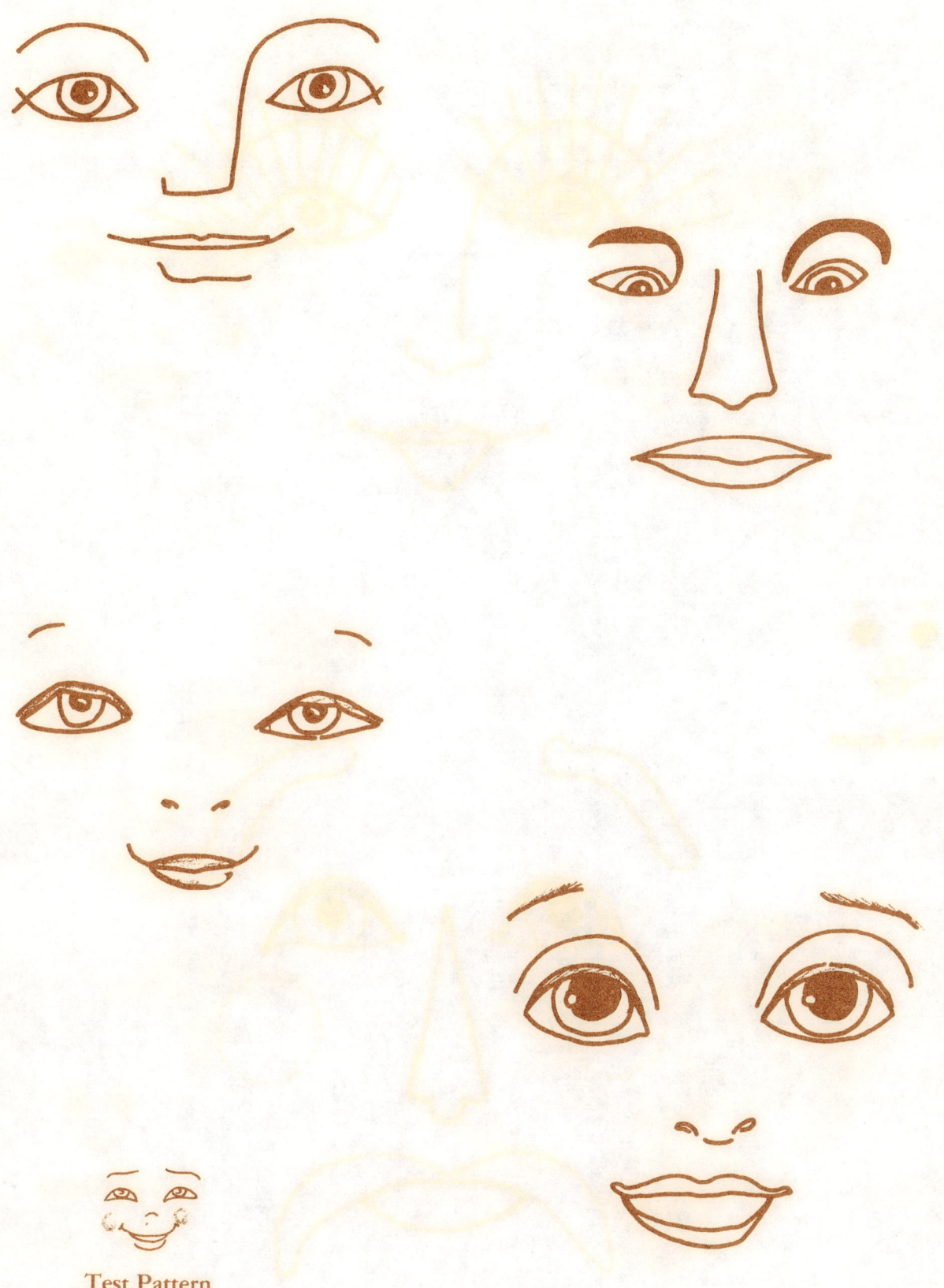

Test Pattern

Plate 7

Test Pattern

Plate 8

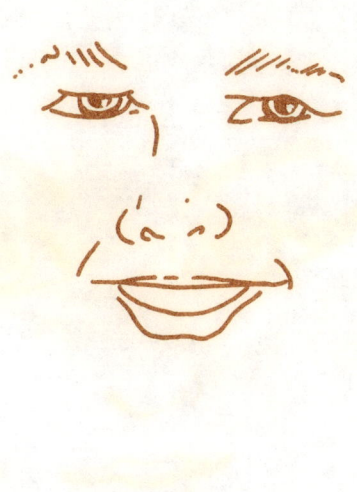

Test Pattern

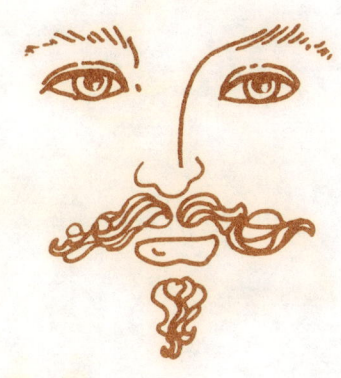
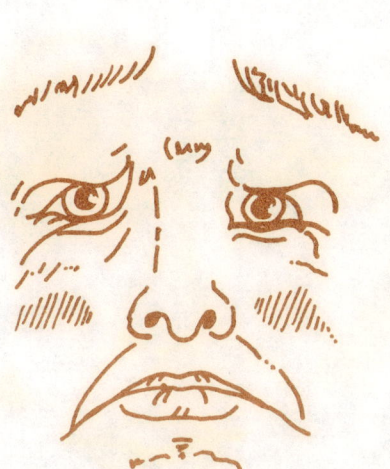

Plate 9

Test Pattern

Plate 10

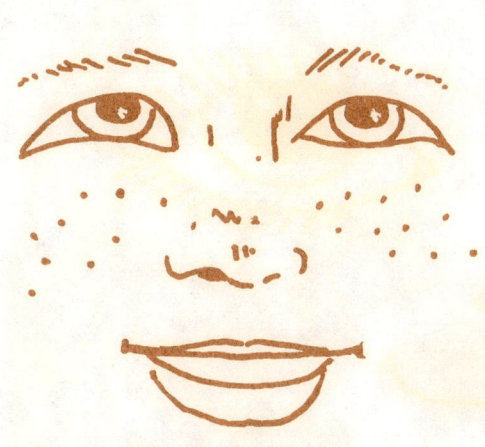

Test Pattern

Plate 11

Test Pattern

Test Pattern

Plate 14

Test Pattern

Plate 15

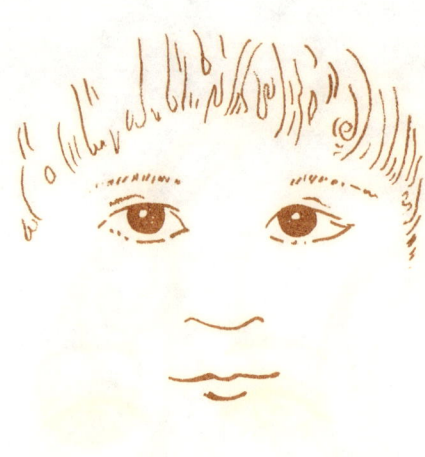

Test Pattern

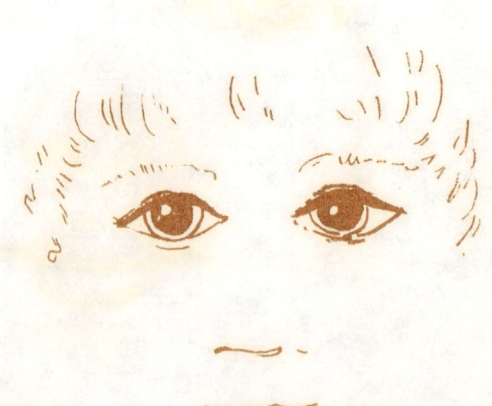

Plate 16

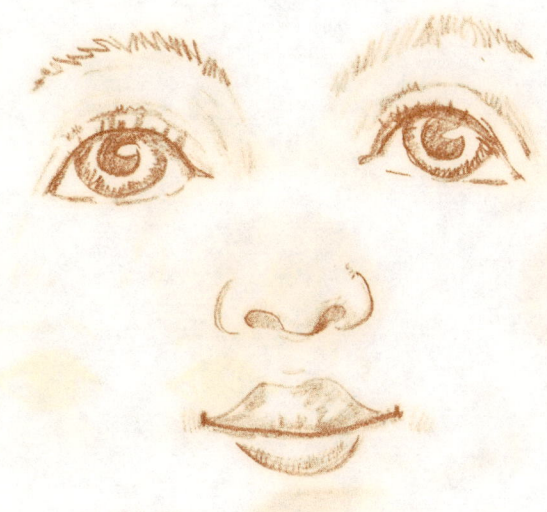

Test Pattern

Plate 17

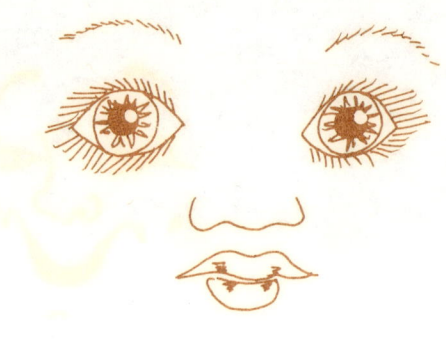

Test Pattern
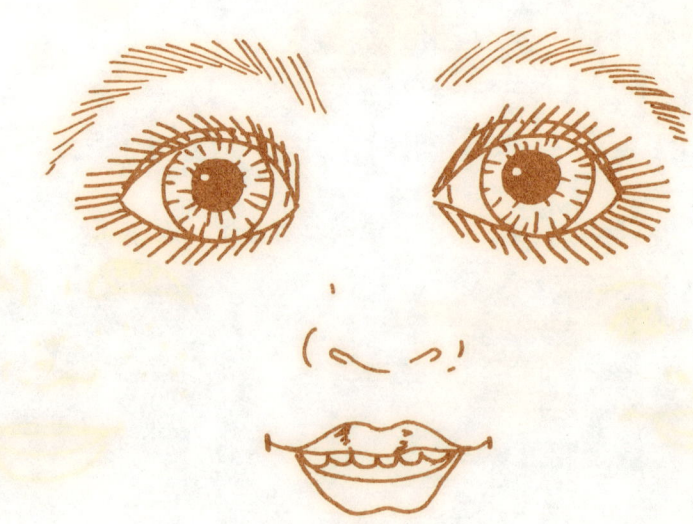

Plate 18

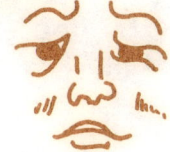

Test Pattern
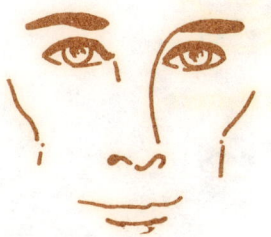

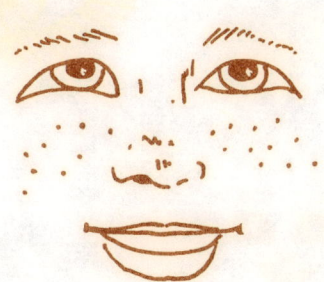

Plate 19

Plate 20   Test Pattern

Test Pattern

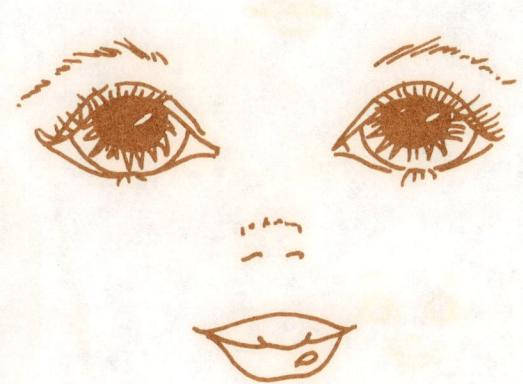

Plate 21

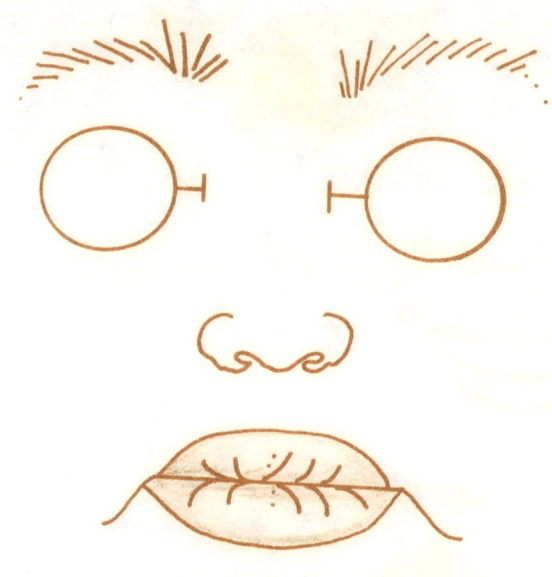

Test Pattern

Plate 22

Test Pattern

Plate 23

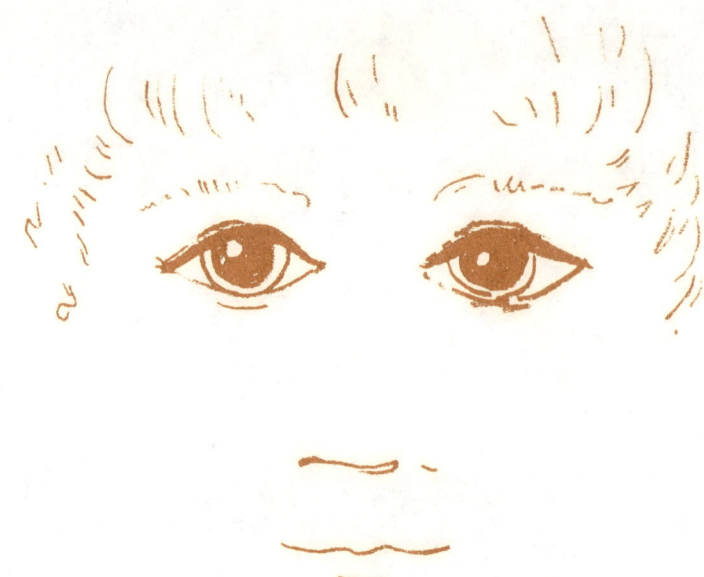

Test Pattern

Plate 24

Needle-sculpting and understructure add dimension and realism to dolls. If the face is to be shaped or placed over padding or other base forms, the fabric should be cut on the bias so that the eyes and other features will pull on the same plane. It is a good idea to test a piece of the material that you are planning to use by stretching it over the form or pattern before actually ironing on the face, to test the direction of pull.

Cut out the face and iron on fabric pattern piece as indicated. If the face is to be appliqued to an existing doll head, allow extra material around the edges. The applique technique is often dramatically successful when polyester stuffing or other forms are inserted beneath the fabric of the face. The fabric face is placed on the head and pinned in place. It is slip stitched in place beginning at center chin and working toward the forehead, on both sides, leaving an opening at the top. The face is then contoured beneath the fabric by inserting pieces of stuffing and tamping in place to produce shaped chin, cheeks and nose.

To choose a face that will fit the doll that you are making, first pick out one that you like and believe the proper size. Check the illustrations of feature placement. Doll patterns usually come with the face position indicated. Note the size of the face and choose one that is comparable. To test for size, trace the face that you choose from the book, or cut it out, leaving a margin all around. Place the tracing or face on the pattern sheet or face area, and hold both up to a light source to check alignment. If the face you have chosen is too large or too small, it will be quite obvious. Small differences are not crucial, but the edges of the printed face must not extend into the seam area, or be too far in any direction from the suggested facial placement, since the result would be distortion of the features when the doll is sewn. The eyes and mouth should be in the same general area on the pattern and the printed face. Doll faces are usually larger than life, feature by feature, but the placement is basically the same. However, every rule is made to be broken, and interesting and exotic effects are sometimes created by the deliberate use of off-scale features and arrangement. In the final analysis the doll maker alone creates his personal vision of the doll. If you are still not certain of the fit, cut the head pattern portion of the doll from a scrap of muslin or cotton. Lay the fabric over the face you have chosen from the book and roughly trace and pencil in the main features. If you have trouble seeing through the fabric, carefully hold fabric and face together against a window pane (daylight) or lighted lamp shade. Baste the trial head together and stuff to check for placement and pencil in any changes or allowances. Arrange yarn or hair around face to simulate hair style planned. Hair placement is almost as important as feature placement, and can totally change the appearance of both face and doll. If the combination is pleasing, remove the stuffing from the trial head for later use, and proceed with the final version of the doll.

The following illustrations show typical feature placement for specific ages. Use the one that most nearly fits the age of the doll that you are making.

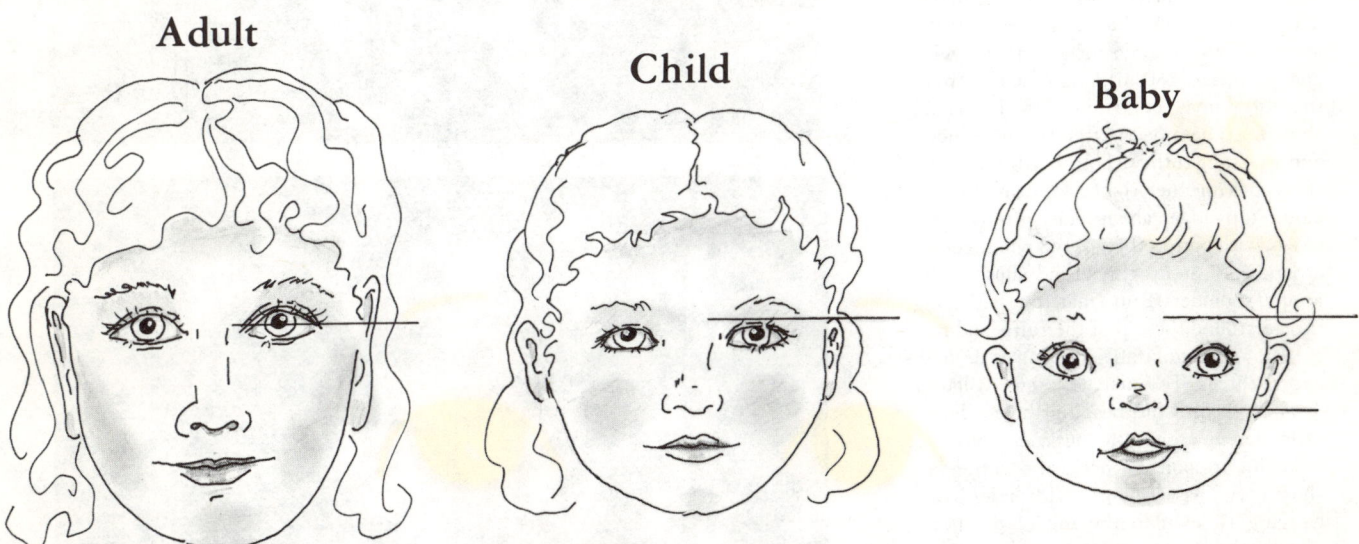

Shadowing indicates placement of contour, cheek and eye color.

Allowing for individual differences, in general babies tend to have heads that are about two-thirds the size of the adult head, with babies heads about six inches (15.2cm) in height and adults approximately nine inches (22.9cm). Proportions change as the child grows. Young children have large heads which are almost twice the proportion of the body as that of the adult, i.e., a one year old child will have a head that is about one-fourth of the total body height, while an adult will have a head that is one-eighth of his total height. These proportions are very useful to the doll maker for depicting age.

When choosing a face PLEASE NOTE EYE PLACEMENT. This is the single most important factor in feature placement, and if done correctly the rest of the face will be in proportion. In the oval that comprises the head, adult eyes are usually placed on an imaginary line that is in the exact center of the head. The bottom of the nose is placed one-half the distance from eyes to bottom of chin. The mouth is placed one-third of the distance between bottom of nose and bottom of chin.

In the child the top of the eye just brushes the half-way mark. The nose and mouth placement are almost the same as those of the adult.

Baby features, *including the eyebrows*, begin at the half-way mark so that all facial detail is on the lower half of the head. The face is divided roughly into four parts, with the eyes one-fourth of the distance down to the chin. The nose is one-half the distance. The mouth three-fourths of the distance.

Instructions for "Sewing Companion"

The concept of the "Sewing Companion" may be used for a number of the faces in this book. Simply use the basic outline and facial plan as a guide for creating other versions of this 19th century notion. For the one pictured, cut out the front and back designs and transfer to fabric. Finish face as desired. The face shown is a combination of acrylic water colors, crewel and embroidery. Cut out (a one-fourth inch [0.65cm] seam allowance is included in the design) and sew around head, leaving bottom open. The neck will seem too small, but the addition of the neck ruffle will compensate. Stuff the head, neck and shoulders. You may wish to insert a rectangular piece of cardboard into the neck to stiffen it when it is stuffed. Stuff shoulders and slip stitch bottom closed. Potpourri added to the stuffing material (polyester preferred) is a delicious and delightful touch. Her costume consists of a strip of fabric 7 inches (17.8cm) wide by 36 inches (91.4cm) long. The top edge may be trimmed with lace or folded over one-half inch (1.3cm) and hemmed. The bottom edge has a gathered ruffle attached, which is 3½ inches (8.9cm) wide and 72 inches (180cm) long. The bottom of the ruffle may be trimmed with lace as shown, or hemmed. After finishing neck, and attaching ruffle to bottom edge, sew two short ends together, right sides facing. Gather along top edge, about one inch (2.5cm) down, with button thread, and pull together around neck. Secure thread and adjust ruffles around shoulders. Run a matching gathering thread around the top of the ruffle and pull gathers to base of doll, adjusting as desired. Secure thread. To finish doll, sew a collar of 3/4 inch (2cm) white beading, threaded with satin ribbon, around the neck. Add bows of matching ribbon to neck and ruffles as shown. A "hair ribbon" with a loop for hanging is sewn to the top of the head. White color pins form the "buttons" on her dress. She also has a pair of scissors on a ribbon around her neck, a cluster of safety pins, several needles, a thimble in a ribbon loop holder and a spool of colorless nylon monofilament thread that can be used with any color fabric. These "Sewing Companions" are thoughtful additions to the guest room, make excellent gifts and bazaar items, and can be made with a variety of materials and trims.

TOP: *"Sewing Companion" concept may be used for many faces in this book. When designing variations, remember to allow space around the edges of the pattern so that doll will not be too skinny when stuffed.*

BOTTOM: *Pincushion design with alternate face. Almost any face in this book might be used for a similar project.*